ANSEL ELGORT

REAL
BiOS

By Marie Morreale

D1483859

Children's Press®
An Imprint of Scholastic Inc.

Photographs ©: cover: Valerie Macon/Getty Images; back cover: Jason Kempin/Getty Images for Paramount Pictures International; 1: Kristin Callahan/Zuma Press; 2, 3: NCP/Getty Images; 4-5: Dave J Hogan/Getty Images for Paramount Pictures International; 6-7: Axelle/Getty Images; 8 left: Patrick McMullan Co./Newscom; 8 right: Steve Granitz/Getty Images; 9: Richard Levine/Alamy Images; 10: Randy Duchaine/Alamy Images; 11: Josiah Kamau/BuzzFoto via Getty Images; 12: Sonia Moskowitz/Zuma Press; 13 top: Batuque/Dreamstime; 13 center left: Nicky Digital/Corbis Images; 13 center right: Ton Koene/Alamy Images; 13 bottom: Lucasfilm/20th Century Fox/The Kobal Collection; 14: Jason Kempin/Getty Images for DCP; 15 top left: Cristina Fumi/Alamy Images; 15 top right: AF archive/Alamy Images; 15 bottom left: Brendan Hunter/iStockphoto; 15 bottom right: Piotr Zajac/Shutterstock, Inc.; 16: Boneau/Bryan-Brown via Getty Images; 18 top: MGM/The Kobal Collection; 18 bottom: MGM/The Kobal Collection; 19 top: Jaap Buitendijk/©Summit Entertainment/Everett Collection; 19 bottom: Photos 12/Alamy Images; 20 left: Ari Perilstein/Getty Images for Variety; 20 right: BT1 WENN Photos/Newscom; 21 top: Andrew Cooper/©Summit Entertainment/Everett Collection; 21 bottom, 22 top: Photos 12/Alamy Images; 22 bottom: C Flanigan/Getty Images; 23 top: David Lobel/Newscom; 23 bottom: AdMedia/Newscom; 24: Photos 12/Alamy Images; 25: Taylor Hill/Getty Images; 26: Photos 12/Alamy Images; 28: Dennis Van Tine/Newscom; 29: Rex USA; 30: Mike Coppola/Getty Images; 31: Kevin Mazur/Getty Images; 32: Stephen Lovekin/Getty Images; 33: NCP/Getty Images; 34: Josiah Kamau/Getty Images; 35: Kevin Mazur/Getty Images; 36 background and throughout: conejota/Thinkstock; 36 pushpins and throughout: seregam/Thinkstock; 36 lined paper and throughout: My Life Graphic/Shutterstock, Inc.; 37 top: Michael C. Gray/Shutterstock, Inc.; 37 bottom: MGM/The Kobal Collection; 37: Kristoffer Tripplaar/Alamy Images; 37 blue paper background and throughout: Nonnakrit/Shutterstock, Inc.; 38 top: Fred Thornhill/Reuters; 38 center: Tinseltown/Shutterstock, Inc.; 38 bottom: Jaguar PS/Shutterstock, Inc.; 39 top: DFree/Shutterstock, Inc.; 39 center: Vera Anderson/Getty Images; 39 bottom: Tinseltown/Shutterstock, Inc.; 40: Douglas Gorenstein/NBC/NBCU Photo Bank via Getty Images; 41: Tim Mosenfelder/Getty Images; 42: Jon Furniss/Corbis Images; 45: JosiahW/Corbis Images.

Library of Congress Cataloging-in-Publication Data
Morreale, Marie.
 Ansel Elgort / by Marie Morreale.
    pages cm. — (Real bios)
 Includes bibliographical references and index.
 ISBN 978-0-531-22377-2 (library binding) — ISBN 978-0-531-22561-5 (pbk.)
 1. Elgort, Ansel, 1994– —Juvenile literature. 2. Actors—United States—Biography—Juvenile literature. I. Title.
 PN2287.E39555M68 2015
 791.4302'8092—dc23 [B]   2015022603

Printed in the United States 113
SCHOLASTIC, CHILDREN'S PRESS, and associated logos are trademarks and/or registered trademarks of Scholastic Inc.

1 2 3 4 5 6 7 8 9 10 R 25 24 23 22 21 20 19 18 17 16

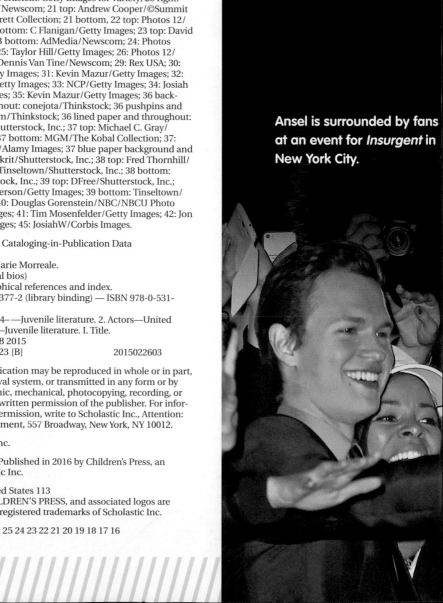

Ansel is surrounded by fans at an event for *Insurgent* in New York City.

MEET ANSEL!

TODAY'S RISING STAR . . . TOMORROW'S SUPERSTAR!

Ansel Elgort has starred in a huge variety of films, from horror and futuristic science fiction to comedies, dramas, and even a **biopic**. He has acted in the off-Broadway play *Regrets*. He has written and performed numerous EDM tracks and has even been signed to two record labels. And he did it all before turning 22 years old!

As you turn the pages of this book, you will learn many more amazing Ansel facts. He's an award-winning painter of miniature characters, a rock climber, and a super basketball fan. More than that, he is truly the boy next door—even though he was raised in New York City. He would rather hang with his family and friends than attend Hollywood hooplas, he would rather shoot hoops with neighbor kids than walk a red carpet, and he would rather wait for just the right film than make one for the money. If you want to know more about Ansel, read on!

DIVERGENT

CONTENTS

Just
Ansel
"I'm just an average guy!"

Ansel smiles for the cameras at a *Men, Women & Children* party.

ANSEL ELGORT—

BORN INTO FAME

FROM BABY PICTURES IN *VOGUE* TO THE BIG SCREEN!

When Ansel Elgort was born in New York City on March 14, 1994, he became part of a very exclusive and creative world. His father, Arthur Elgort, is a legendary fashion photographer. For more than 30 years, Arthur's work has appeared in hundreds of magazines. He is best known for his beautiful covers and fashion shoots in *Vogue*. On top of that, Ansel's mother, Grethe Barrett Holby, is a well-respected opera director. Ansel's older sister, Sophie, followed in their father's footsteps and became a photographer. His older brother, Warren, is a filmmaker.

Ansel's first brush with fame came when he was a little boy. Arthur often included Ansel in his *Vogue* fashion shoots. By the time he started school, Ansel was already very comfortable being photographed.

Perfect Day
"Music, good food, long drives with friends."

Famed photographer Arthur Elgort joins his son Ansel at the premiere of The Fault in Our Stars.

Ansel and his mom, Grethe Barrett Holby, at the Oscars

He was also interested in the performing arts. "Growing up, I was a ridiculous ball of energy who spoke in weird voices and loved to act out," Ansel told *People* magazine. "And I wanted to be a lot of things. . . . [My parents] were both totally behind me when they heard I wanted to be a performer."

> "JUST BE YOURSELF. YOU'LL NEVER BE ABLE TO PLEASE EVERYONE. THE PEOPLE [WHO] MATTER WILL RESPECT YOU."

Ansel fans might be surprised at his first onstage experience. "I realized I wanted to be a performer when I was about nine," he revealed to *Parade* magazine. "I did ballet and went out on stage for the first time as a ballet dancer and I loved being on stage and then later that turned into wanting to be an actor."

Ansel's interest in acting led him to enter the legendary Fiorello H. LaGuardia High School of Music & Art and Performing Arts—the same school where the movie *Fame* was set. "I always did workshops," Ansel told *Interview* magazine. "I would be at theater camp, doing shows, or after-school programs. Then I was doing shows in school. It was nonstop. I was never not in a show from ages 11 until 18. It was a great atmosphere but also a professional kind of atmosphere. When I finally went into the professional world, I felt ready. I was prepared for work."

Boo Hoo "I love to cry. It's great!"

Ansel spent many of his teenage years at the LaGuardia High School.

Though Ansel thrived on the stage, he was definitely not an all-work-no-play kind of guy. He was a little bit goofy, with a taste of daring, and a free spirit. In other words, he was a typical teenager. "On an average Saturday, I would have just a sleepover with my best friend [Jordan Berman], who I've been best friends with since pre-school," he revealed to Complex.com. "We'd go to a pancake shop, and then go paint pictures for a few hours. Then we'd go rock climbing at Brooklyn Boulders before going back into the city. If we still weren't tired, we'd go to Trinity Boxing Club and box. After that, we'd go back to his house or my house and eat cheese wedges or cereal bars and watch *Hell's Kitchen* or *Jersey Shore*."

Whenever Ansel is home in New York, he loves a good rock climb at Brooklyn Boulders.

All In
"I put 100 percent into everything!"

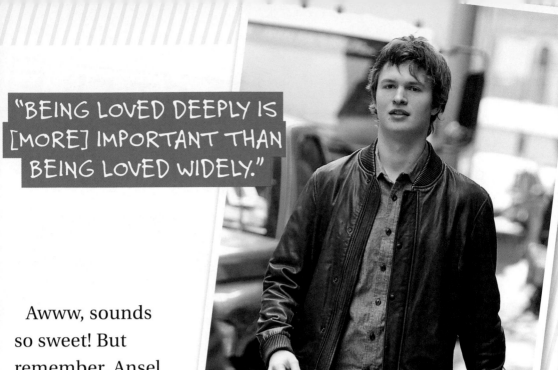

Ansel loves the hustle and bustle of New York City streets.

Awww, sounds so sweet! But remember, Ansel was also a little bit edgier than most kids his age. There were times he took his adventurous ways a bit too far. "Jordan and I used to throw eggs off my roof and hit cars," Ansel confessed to *Seventeen* magazine. "We got in trouble with the police when I was 15. They came to our door. I told my dad, 'We were throwing eggs off the roof and you were out of town and they got really mad at us and said if we did it again we would get in trouble, but we're never going to do it again.' I said it all in one sentence. He was like, 'Okay.'"

Ansel kept his word—he didn't want to let his father down. As for life at LaGuardia, Ansel found he fit in better than he had in middle school. "I was always kind of popular," he explained to *Seventeen*. "I wasn't really nerdy, but I always had really weird hobbies. Every Friday night, Jordan and I would go to the miniatures shop until nine when it closed, and then we would go rock climbing. My parents trusted me because I was honest with them. Also, I'm the youngest, so my parents were just over it. We didn't really go to parties. Okay, maybe we were kind of nerdy. But in my school, there was no such thing as being nerdy. If you were the

THE BASICS

EDM DJ
Ansølo is Ansel's DJ name!

NAME: Ansel Elgort

NICKNAME: "My brother would call me An Solo. And that's now my DJ, my **producer**, name."

EDM DJ NAME: Ansølo

BIRTHPLACE: New York, New York

CURRENT RESIDENCE: Williamsburg, Brooklyn

ROOMMATE: Pierce Fulton, also an EDM DJ/ producer

HEIGHT: 6'4"

DANCE SCHOOL: Stagedoor Manor summer camp

HIGH SCHOOL: Fiorello H. LaGuardia High School of Music & Art and Performing Arts

INSTRUMENT: Trumpet

SURPRISING FACT: He paints miniature figures

TWITTER FOLLOWERS: More than 3.1 million

INSTAGRAM FOLLOWERS: More than 5.2 million

VINE FOLLOWERS: 2.3 million

FAN HANDLE: Anselites

Ansel may have painted a miniature of *Star Wars*'s **Han Solo**, but the character had nothing to do with his DJ name.

CELEB CRUSH: Charlize Theron

KARAOKE SONG: "Easy" by the Commodores

lead in the musical, you were the coolest kid in school."

According to Ansel, being a Big Apple kid really helped him develop as an actor. "Growing up in New York City was so helpful because you end up never being in one bubble, you experience people and communities," he said to *Parade* magazine. "There's so much diversity and that's so important—especially as an actor. I feel like I can bring so many characters alive because of that."

And Ansel was soon able to prove that he was truly an actor!

FACT FILE

FAVORITES

THE FAULT IN OUR STARS
"THIS BOOK AND MOVIE TELL THE TRUTH."

SPORTS: Basketball, rock climbing

SPORTS TEAM: New York Knicks

AUTHOR: John Green (The Fault in Our Stars)

EMOJI: The Big Tongue

SUPERHERO: Superman—Ansel would love to be able to fly

CLASSIC ACTORS: Paul Newman, Marlon Brando, James Dean

CURRENT ACTORS: Tom Hardy, Christian Bale

BOOK: The Fault in Our Stars

MUSICIAN: DJ Mat Zo

TYPE OF MUSIC: EDM/House

HOLLYWOOD ERA: "The '50s—the whole greaser time in Hollywood."

DATE: A walk in NYC's Central Park

VIDEO GAME: Grand Theft Auto

HOLIDAY: Christmas

SOCIAL MEDIA: Skype, Instagram

FILMS: The Lord of the Rings series

COLOR: Dark blue

CHILDHOOD TOY: Playmobil

SINGER: Adam Lambert

ANSEL WOULD LOVE TO BE GANDALF IN *THE LORD OF THE RINGS* FOR ONE DAY.

Alexis Bledel and Ansel star in the Off-Broadway play *Regrets*.

ANSEL
REACHES FOR
THE STARS

THE NYC KID TAKES ON HOLLYWOOD!

Ansel received much praise for performances in student productions, but his professional debut wasn't so well received. At age 18, his big break was appearing in the Off-Broadway play *Regrets*. His costar was Alexis Bledel. Unfortunately, the *New York Times* wasn't so impressed. "Mr. Elgort is stiffer than his crisp blue jeans in the crucial role of Caleb," the reviewer wrote. "Hitching his thumbs into his pockets and striking [James] Dean-like poses, he looks the model of a handsome but troubled 1950s youth, but brings absolutely no spark or suggestion of inner life to the role."

Though the review must have been disappointing to Ansel, little did he know that a mere two years later, he would receive rave reviews for playing another

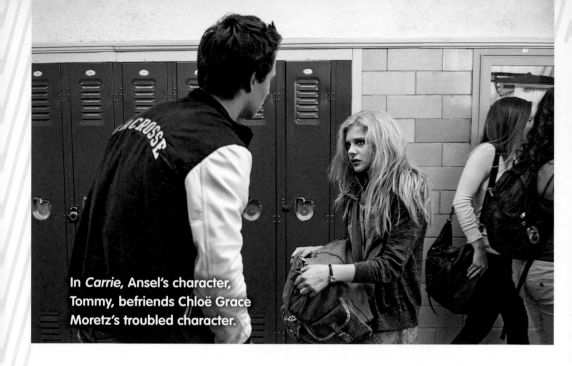

In *Carrie*, Ansel's character, Tommy, befriends Chloë Grace Moretz's troubled character.

character named Caleb. Of course, *that* Caleb was the star of the *Divergent* series. Before that, Ansel made his film debut in the 2013 horror flick *Carrie*. Ansel was up for one of the leads in the film, Tommy Ross. Believe it or not, Ansel didn't walk in and get the role after his first **audition** . . . or the second . . . or the third. He had to audition seven times! "I just kept coming back and

Ansel's Timeline

Ansel's Road to Fame

MARCH 27, 2012
Ansel makes his Off-Broadway debut in *Regrets*

OCTOBER 18, 2013
Ansel stars as Tommy Ross in *Carrie*

MARCH 21, 2014
Ansel stars as Caleb Prior in *Divergent*

doing the same thing over and over again," he shared with *Interview* magazine. "I guess they just wanted to see if I was consistent. I was a total nobody. I wouldn't have hired me to be the lead in that movie, either."

Luckily Ansel's performance proved that he was no longer a "nobody." After *Carrie*, Ansel was looking for his next role. "I was living with my parents, who were very supportive," he told MTV News. "I was just making tapes all the time in my stairwell."

In *Divergent*, Caleb (Ansel) and Tris (Shailene Woodley) learn the rules.

APRIL 21, 2014
Ansel's first song as DJ Ansølo, "Unite," is released

JUNE 6, 2014
Ansel stars as Augustus Waters in *The Fault in Our Stars*

JUNE 23, 2014
Ansel is announced to play the lead role in the upcoming biopic *Van Cliburn*

JULY 21, 2014
Ansølo's second single, "Totem," is released

Seven months after *Carrie*, Ansel's agent sent him to audition for the upcoming *Divergent* series. "I auditioned for Four," he continued with MTV. "We did a few takes and it wasn't really working—it was okay, whatever." Theo James got the role of Four, and Ansel was one of the first to praise the choice. "I don't think you could've gotten a better Four," he shared with MTV News. "He's so good looking and he's so scary at the same time." While Ansel didn't get the role of Four, he did win the part of Caleb. He couldn't have been happier. The role was an actor's dream. "Caleb's really different from me," Ansel told *Teen Vogue*. "He is battling himself on whether or not he believes in what he stands for. He's a young person and young people latch on to something to feel like they have some sort of purpose. . . . He's not a leading man, which is cool."

JULY 28, 2014
Ansel wins Fan Favorite Actor—Male and Best On-Screen Couple (with Shailene Woodley) at The Young Hollywood Awards

The Divergent Series: Insurgent stars (l to r): Shailene Woodley, Theo James, and Ansel Elgort.

Being cast as Caleb in *Divergent* meant that Ansel would also star in the sequels, *The Divergent Series: Insurgent*, *The Divergent Series: Allegiant Part 1*, and *The Divergent Series: Allegiant Part 2*. That was a lot of job security, but Ansel wasn't satisfied. In between *Divergent* and *Insurgent*, he was thrilled when he was asked to audition for the movie version of John Green's

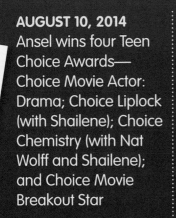

AUGUST 10, 2014
Ansel wins four Teen Choice Awards—Choice Movie Actor: Drama; Choice Liplock (with Shailene); Choice Chemistry (with Nat Wolff and Shailene); and Choice Movie Breakout Star

AUGUST 2014
Ansølo plays the main stage at the Electric Zoo festival

OCTOBER 17, 2014:
Ansel stars as Tim Mooney in *Men, Women & Children*

Ansel and Shailene reunite as costars in *The Fault in Our Stars*.

best-selling novel *The Fault in Our Stars*. If he won the role of Augustus, he would be working with his *Divergent* costar Shailene Woodley. Even Green was a bit concerned about that. When it came time to choose who would get the part, Ansel told *Teen Vogue*, "John Green was like, 'Please be anyone but the girl's brother from *Divergent*.'"

FEBRUARY 22, 2015
Ansel and Chloë Grace Moretz present the award for Best Visual Effects at the 2015 Oscars

MARCH 14, 2015
Ansølo headlines a show at Pacha NYC—it was Ansel's 21st birthday

MARCH 20, 2015
The Divergent Series: Insurgent is released

Even with his reservations about pairing up Shailene and Ansel again, Green was amazed at Ansel's audition—he just knew that Ansel was Gus! Of course, Ansel had done his homework and read *The Fault in Our Stars* before he met with *TFIOS*'s producers.

As a matter of fact, he told the *Guardian* newspaper, "I wasn't aware of the book until I was auditioning for it, but, yes, I read it before I auditioned. . . . I was very affected. I cried a bunch. I really,

Ansel and singer Joe Jonas enjoy the 2014 U.S. Open Tennis Championships. Some fans had selfie fun with them.

APRIL 12, 2015
Ansel wins Best Duo (with Shailene) for *TFIOS* at the MTV Movie Awards

MARCH 18, 2016
The Divergent Series: Allegiant Part 1 is released

MARCH 24, 2017
The Divergent Series: Allegiant Part 2 is released

Ansel and Kaitlyn Dever in
Men, Women & Children.

really liked it. When I read it, I didn't see myself as Gus . . . yet, which is a good thing. I think that when you first read material or you first read a script or story and know you might be playing a part, it's important not to see yourself because it should be a challenge enough that it doesn't come easy. I think Gus was always going to be a challenge and that's important. Characters I want to play are challenges to me."

The important thing was that Ansel understood his character. "Augustus is quirky, weird, and nerdy," he told *Teen Vogue*. "Augustus seems almighty. But clearly there's stuff underneath that. He finally finds something that he thinks matters, which is Hazel [Shailene's character]. Whatever she likes, he likes too."

In his typical low-key manner, Ansel credits *TFIOS* for his popularity. "If I hadn't played Augustus Waters or been in any movies, no one would care about me at all," Ansel told TheVent.tv. "No one would be screaming 'Ansel' at the MTV Movie Awards. So, fame's not going to go to my head because I know what's important. This is not happening because I'm special. It's happening because of the book and the film."

Ansel has become a respected actor with fans and filmmakers alike. You only have to look at his upcoming films—*Men, Women & Children*; *The Divergent Series*: *Allegiant Parts 1 & 2*; *November Criminals*; *Baby Driver*; and *Van Cliburn*—to see that his career is going only one way: UP!

Shailene and Ansel attend the NYC premiere of *The Fault in Our Stars.*

"WHEN GIRLS SCREAM MY NAME AND START CRYING, I BLUSH LIKE CRAZY."

Ansel and Shailene on the set of *The Fault in Our Stars.*

ANSEL WANTS YOU TO GET TO KNOW HIM

QUOTES, QUOTES, AND MORE QUOTES!

Ansel muses about his films, his family, and his fans. Bet you didn't know he considers himself a goofy kinda guy . . . or that he's a secret romantic . . . or who makes him starstruck. Read on to find out more.

On what he learned from *The Fault in Our Stars* . . . "I want people to take away hope from this movie. Nat [Wolff] who plays Isaac said someone came up to him after the movie and said, 'I want to call everyone who I love and tell them I love them.' That's the message: to appreciate what's in front of you."

On dating . . . "I like to go on really nice dates. I've made some money, but I don't spend it on anything

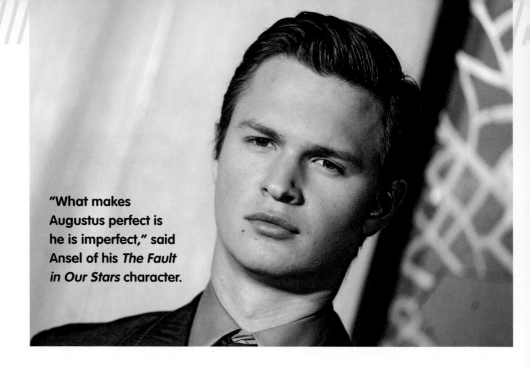

"What makes Augustus perfect is he is imperfect," said Ansel of his *The Fault in Our Stars* character.

besides my rent. But I go to nice dinners. And I like to go with a girl. I prefer being with a girlfriend long-term. I prefer to be with someone I can trust. I'm more into that."

On his goofy side . . . "I'm a total goof. When I'm being really comfortable with my friends, I can be very goofy. I'm open with how I feel about someone."

Bullies
Ansel says to just ignore them!

On everyone being equal . . . "I almost find that now if you're not accepting, it's a big problem . . . I really hope in my heart that the world can accept, like truly and deeply from the core, so there can be a true change in the way the world is. I mean, everyone's allowed to have their own opinion, but there really shouldn't be people who don't accept everyone. I think that's really stupid."

On how to handle bullies . . . "I was bullied in middle school and hated it. But instead of focusing on bullies, you should focus on the things you love. You'll find other people who share your interests and they'll become your friends."

Ansel at the 2015 Ultra Music Festival in Miami.

On his dating history . . . "I like relationships. I don't play games, like waiting to text. If I like you, I'm going for it!"

On being an actor . . . "I didn't grow up wanting to be a Hollywood guy. I grew up just wanting to be an actor. In fact, I just wanted to be on Broadway. That was my dream, and then that sort of changed because I got in a movie."

On his idols . . .

"I got starstruck not by someone who is famous, but by someone who's famous in the miniature painting community. When I was a kid, I used to paint miniatures. There were famous people in the miniature community from forums online. I went to some big event and I saw them in real life and I was so starstruck."

Opening night for Ansel's Off-Broadway debut, *Regrets*

Ansel gives Taylor Swift a hug at the 2014 American Music Awards.

On his extracurricular activities . . . "From 12 to 17, those years of my life were all about miniatures. They're made for gaming—you build them and paint them. I've won painting competitions. My trophies are in my bathroom above my toilet. But when I was 17, I got into producing music and that took over my time. I love writing music. It's my favorite thing to do now."

Ansel's dad, Arthur, has given him photo tips all his life!

On his photographer father . . . "He has always just been like, 'Do what you love and don't worry about money—the money will come later. Whatever you love to do, put your entire self behind it and you will be successful, because most people are scared to do that.' He did that with photography and it worked pretty well for him, and it worked pretty well for me so far with acting, so I'm really grateful for that advice."

On personal vs. private . . . "There are big parts of my life that I don't share. I don't share myself eating dinner with my family, I don't talk about who I'm dating. That's private, that's me. The business of life and the real life are totally different things, and just to keep your sanity, and to keep who you are sacred—because I think part of being an artist is being who you are and expressing who you are and being an actor is being someone that people can relate to. You need to keep them separate."

Fans = Selfies. That's a lesson Ansel has learned.

On the time he turned his phone off . . . "It was really nice. I was able to just hang out with some friends and I convinced them to turn off their phones too. To be completely honest about how the break went, I did turn on my phone for about 10 minutes a day just to check my e-mail and make sure nothing terrible was happening. It was a nice feeling. Having that time off was super nice. The thing is that I didn't really miss it."

Wonder what's in Ansel's bag? Can't be a mall haul in NYC!

SHAILENE KNEW BEFORE ANSEL THAT HE WON THE GUS ROLE IN THE FAULT IN OUR STARS.

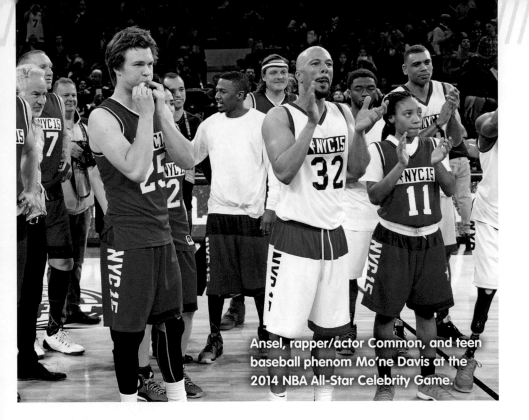

Ansel, rapper/actor Common, and teen baseball phenom Mo'ne Davis at the 2014 NBA All-Star Celebrity Game.

On everyday Ansel . . . "I try to act like the guy everyone thinks I am. If I'm talking to someone, I'll be cool and sweet and flash 'em my best smile, whereas in real life I'm a total goofball. I play video games and sit at my computer and make music all day."

On being a role model . . . "I'm happy to be a role model because I think I can do it over other people. I think my parents raised me well. And I'm pretty straight edge. All my friends make fun of me for being straight edge. . . . I'm really focused always on the prize. I want to keep creating and making important things and that's what I want Ansel Elgort to be about."

ANSEL'S LOOK BOOK

FACTS! QUOTES! SILLY STORIES! . . . EVERY BIT OF TRIVIA YOU NEED TO KNOW!

ANSEL'S PLAYLIST

EDM Dream
Ansel played the main stage at NYC's Electric Zoo festival

MISSY ELLIOTT'S "LOSE CONTROL"
This was Ansel's fave when he was in fifth grade. He would love to do a remix.

THE COMMODORES' "EASY"
Ansel loves to sing it at karaoke nights.

MAT ZO
Ansel loves anything by this British producer/DJ.

"I DREAMED A DREAM" FROM LES MISÉRABLES
Ansel loves Broadway musicals.

"THE FISHIN' HOLE"
The theme song from *The Andy Griffith Show* is one of Ansel's favorite tunes.

"IF I HAD YOU" BY ADAM LAMBERT
Ansel thinks Adam is the best singer ever.

YUM, YUM, YUM!

Ansel is a definite foodie . . . check it out!

FAVORITE FOOD
SUSHI

PIZZA CITY
NEW YORK

TOP CHEF
"I MAKE REALLY GOOD
OVER-EASY EGGS.
I THINK I SPENT A YEAR
MAKING EGGS EVERY DAY,
AND I JUST WANTED TO
PERFECT THE OVER EASY."

PIZZA TOPPING
PEPPERONI

GUILTY PLEASURE
GIRL SCOUT COOKIES

OOPS!

Ansel was really excited about winning
the role of Tommy Ross in *Carrie*, and he
loved sharing his good fortune . . . even
with strangers! One day in 2013, Ansel
was on a New York subway. A fellow
passenger was actually watching *Carrie*
on his iPhone, and Ansel was in the scene. "I was so
excited. . . . I tapped him on the shoulder. He looked at
me like I was crazy, and then I'm like, 'No, no, no, that's
me.' And he goes 'What?' and takes out his earbuds.
And I'm like, 'That's me right there!'"

YOU
WILL
KNOW
HER
NAME

CARRIE

ANSEL & CELEB PALS CHIT-CHAT

Ansel on *The Fault in Our Stars* and *Divergent* costar Shailene Woodley: "Shailene is honest with people . . . she's not fake, she's a real friend because of that to me. I learned a lot about her because she's so open. She's a totally open soul to me and I'm a totally open soul to her. . . . Shailene is a super-generous person. She's very idealistic and not a conformist at all."

Ansel on his *Carrie* and *November Criminals* costar Chloë Grace Moretz: "Oh, gosh, Chloë is very sweet. We became really close during *Carrie* because we are similar in age."

Ansel on Asa Butterfield: "At Comic-Con, two days before [my] *Teen Vogue* shoot, Asa Butterfield and I clicked and became total best friends . . . over house music!"

Nat Wolff on Ansel: During the filming of *TFIOS*, Nat remembered, "Ansel and I had apartments right next to each other, so I would play him my new songs with my brother [Alex Wolff] because my brother would be sending me rough mixes of our songs from the studio. And Ansel would be playing different EDM tracks that he'd do, so we'd be going back and forth, which was fun and cool."

John Green on Ansel: "I think he's the absolute revelation in this movie [*TFIOS*]. Everyone knows Shailene is prodigiously talented, but Ansel is just wonderful. He is my Gus."

Shailene Woodley on Ansel: "Every single day [Ansel] looks at the world with a new set of eyes. He is the most creative person I've ever met. This dude is a producer. He paints miniatures and wins contests painting miniatures, which is insane. He's a ballet dancer. He is literally the most creative person."

FUN FIRSTS

CD HE OWNED: "The first music I was ever into was show tunes. *Oklahoma, The King and I*, and that says something about who I am now."

THEATER SHOW HE PERFORMED IN: *The Nutcracker* ballet

LATE-NIGHT TALK SHOW APPEARANCE: *The Tonight Show Starring Jimmy Fallon* in March 2014.

FAVORITE MOVIE: "My favorite movie growing up was *Billy Madison*. It was just really funny and crude and it had bad words in it and funny parts and I loved it!"

NATIONAL ATTENTION: He modeled for a fashion shoot in *Teen Vogue* in 2009 and was featured in their 2013 Young Hollywood Rising Stars article.

TIME MEETING SHAILENE WOODLEY: "My first meeting with Shailene, she comes over and gives me a big hug. And I think I was taken by surprise a little bit, and I didn't hug her back that much."

> "I'M ONLY TRYING TO PUT OUT REALLY GREAT MUSIC THAT OTHER ARTISTS WILL RESPECT ME FOR."

Ansel performs as his EDM persona, DJ Ansølo.

DJ ANSØLO RULES

With blockbusters like the Divergent series and *The Fault in Our Stars* to his credit, you might wonder how Ansel finds time for a whole other career as the dance music producer and DJ Ansølo. Well, he does! He recalled, "I started going to these shows when I was 16. I went to Skrillex before he was big when he wasn't even a headliner. I saw Avicii when he played early on in the day at the festival, before 'Levels' came out. I'm a huge dance music fan."

Ansel started out by posting his tracks to his SoundCloud account. Later, he signed with the EDM labels Staar Traxx and Size Records. He has released tracks such as "Unite" and "Totem," which reached number nine on iTunes dance charts. He also makes club and festival appearances whenever he can. Ansel is respected by his fellow DJs and producers.

What big producer is calling Ansel on the phone now?

ANSEL'S
FOCUS ON SUCCESS
HE DOES EXACTLY WHAT HE LOVES

"There are so many things to be lucky for," Ansel told an interviewer from the *Guardian* when they were discussing *The Fault in Our Stars*. "Lucky to be healthy, lucky to be, like, beautiful. Lucky to be living in America. It's like . . . it's crazy. Feel like I have more luck than 99.999% of people in the whole world. I'm a lucky [guy]!"

Of course, luck can be a fleeting thing, but Ansel is very grounded, both personally and professionally. He has always had the support of his family, and he's put in the hard work to establish a career for a long time to come. He's earned the respect of his peers as well as the producers, directors, and studio bigwigs who put in the money to make movies. Ansel is grateful for his good luck, but he learned from his father that success means loving what you do and preparing yourself for the job. "I'm not really too worried about what I'm gonna do next, because I just think of my career as, like, having sixty years ahead of me," he told *GQ*. "I still have my entire twenties to make movies. I'm in no hurry. I know I'm going to work. I'm not antsy. There's no reason to be in five mediocre movies a year when I can be in one great movie."

> "IT'S REALLY NICE WHEN PEOPLE RECOGNIZE YOUR WORK . . . SO I'M REALLY GRATEFUL."

Indeed, Ansel has a plan A, a plan B, and maybe even a plan C. "You can't really mess up in life that much if you want to be super successful," he told gurl.com. "I'm realizing that every step of the way. Being in that [school] show that got me my manager, who got me a play, who got me agents, who got me movies. . . . If I got suspended [from school] for doing something dumb, I wouldn't be where I am . . . I don't know where I'd be. You have to control yourself and not do stupid things. I know it sounds simple, but like . . . there's so many opportunities to do stupid things in life, and you can't really do them if you really have a goal. If you want to chase something, you have to be focused on it and not let little distractions get [to] you."

Ansel not only talks the talk, but he walks the walk. By the age of 21, he had been in five major blockbusters. That kind of success could go to his head. But that hasn't happened to Ansel. He knows that being focused is his way to the next part of his career. He's not picking silly movies just to make money and keep his name in the **tabloids**. He tries to keep his personal life simple, normal, and private. He's even chosen not to be closer to the Hollywood life. "I'm not going to move to L.A. and spend too much time at fancy parties," he told *Teen Vogue*. "New York is where my friends and family are. For me to make all new friends right now would be a bad decision."

> "I TRY TO BE AN ARTIST, NOT JUST AN ACTOR WHO DOES OTHER THINGS ON THE SIDE."

Ansel has big plans for himself, and they include doing what he loves, whether it be acting, music, or even taking time off to go rock climbing! He wants to try new things, too. "I don't want to only play the leading man for the rest of my life," he told *Teen Vogue*. "And even though Augustus is a leading man, he's not the typical leading man. He's nerdy, he has one leg, he has cancer. My favorite actors are people like Tom Hardy and Christian Bale, who can play characters and also be leading men. I want to play both my whole career, so the fact that I'm able to do both now is awesome."

Ansel has other plans, too. "I want to do a musical," he told *Seventeen*. "I want to dance. I want to do a remake of *On the Waterfront*. . . . Imagine if you could do only what you wanted and be successful."

"TRY AS MANY THINGS AS YOU CAN."

Ansel poses for a 2014 *Town and Country* photo shoot by his father.

Resources

ARTICLES

Entertainment Weekly, May 9, 2014
"How the Greatest Romance Story of This Decade Made it to the Screen."

Parade.com, May 29, 2014
"Shailene Woodley and Ansel Elgort Get Emotional in *The Fault in Our Stars*: 'It Felt So Real.'"

Seventeen, April 2014
"I Like Girls Who Have a Passion!"

Teen Vogue, April 2015
"Best Date Ever!"

Teen Vogue, September 2015
"Ansel Elgort on Movies, Music, and What He Would Do If He Was Taylor Swift."

Facts for Now

Visit this Scholastic Web site for more information on **Ansel Elgort**: www.factsfornow.scholastic.com
Enter the keywords **Ansel Elgort**

Glossary

audition *(aw-DISH-uhn)* give a short performance to compete for a part in a play, film, or television show

biopic *(BYE-oh-pik)* a movie that details the life story of a real person

producer *(pruh-DOO-sur)* someone who creates electronic music

tabloids *(TAB-loidz)* newspapers that contain brief articles and many pictures; the pictures and articles are often intended to stir up interest or excitement

Index

Acknowledgments

Page 5: Just Ansel: *J-14* December 2014
Page 7: Perfect Day: *Seventeen* December 2014
Page 8: Just be yourself: Twitter, August 2014
Page 8: Growing up: *People* June 9, 2014
Page 8: Ballet: *Parade* May 29, 2014
Page 9: Workshops: *Interview* June 2015
Page 9: Boo Hoo: gurl.com September 2014
Page 10: Typical Saturday: *J-14* June 2014
Page 10: All In: *Seventeen* September 2013
Page 11: NYC Streets: Twitter June 2014
Page 11: Egging cars: Seventeen.com March 16, 2015
Page 12: LaGuardia: *Seventeen* April 2015
Page 13: Nickname: J-14.com June 11, 2014
Page 14: NYC kid: *Parade* May 29, 2014
Page 14: Truth: Thebigissue.com July 6, 2014
Page 15: Hollywood Era: *Interview* 2015
Page 17: *Regrets* review: *New York Times* March 27, 2012
Page 18: *Carrie* audition: *Interview* July 2014
Page 19: Between *Carrie* & *Divergent*: MTV News March 3, 2014
Page 20: Four: MTV News

March 3, 2014
Page 20: Caleb: *TeenVogue* April 2015
Page 22: Fave Quote: *Seventeen* September 2013
Page 22: John Green audition: *TeenVogue* June /July 2014
Page 23: *TFIOS* audition: *Guardian* June 19, 2014
Page 24: Augustus: *TeenVogue* June/July 2014
Page 25: Fame: *J-14* December 2014
Page 25: Girls scream: *People* June 9, 2014
Page 27: On *TFIOS*: Theguardian.com June 19, 2014
Page 28: Augusts perfect: Thebigissue.com July 6, 2014
Page 28: Goofy side: elle .com February 18, 2015
Page 28: On everyone being equal: MTV News April 17, 2015
Page 29: On handling bullies: *Seventeen* September 2013
Page 30: On romantic thing: *Seventeen* December 2014
Page 30: On dating: *Seventeen* September 2013
Page 30: On acting: Ryanseacrest.com March 11, 2015
Page 30: On his idols: gurl .com September 5, 2014
Page 31: On extracurricular activities: *Seventeen* April

2015
Page 32: On his father: *J-14* June 2014
Page 33: On personal vs. private: *Vogue* October 2014
Page 33: Friends: *J-14* December 2014
Page 34: On his phone off: gurl.com October 13, 2014
Page 35: On everyday Ansel: *TeenVogue* April 2015
Page 35: On being a role model: *Guardian* June 12, 2014
Page 36: Playlist: *GQ* March 2015
Page 37: Top Chef: gurl.com September 5, 2014
Page 37: NYC Subway: *Bop* October 2014
Page 38: Ansel on Shailene Woodley: *Parade* May 29, 2014
Page 38: Ansel on Chloë Grace Moretz: *Seventeen* September 2013
Page 38: Ansel on Asa Butterfield: *TeenVogue* September 2013
Page 39: Nat Wolff on Ansel: Glamour.com September 16, 2014
Page 39: John Green on Ansel: MTV News June 7, 2014
Page 39: Shailene Woodley on Ansel: People.com May 5, 2014

Page 40: First CD: *Parade* May 29, 2014
Page 40: Favorite movie: *Parade* May 29, 2014
Page 40: Meeting Shailene Woodley: MTV News March 3, 2013
Page 40: Great music: *GQ* March 2015
Page 41: DJ start: gurl.com October 13, 2014
Page 42: Lucky: *Guardian* June 12, 2014
Page 43: Life pretty good: *J-14* 2015
Page 43: Career ahead: *GQ* December 2014
Page 43: Can't mess up: gurl.com October 12, 2014
Page 43: People recognize your work: People.com 2014
Page 44: Staying in NYC: *TeenVogue* April 2015
Page 44: Artist: *Seventeen* September 2013
Page 45: Try many things: *Seventeen Malaysia* December 2014
Page 45: Leading men: *TeenVogue* March 2014
Page 45: Musical: *Seventeen* April 2015

About the Author

Marie Morreale is the author of many official and unofficial celebrity biographies. She attended New York University as an English/creative writing major and began her writing and editorial career in New York City. As the editor of teen/music magazines *Teen Machine* and *Jam!*, she covered TV, film, and music personalities and interviewed superstars such as Michael Jackson, Britney Spears, and Justin Timberlake/*NSYNC. Morreale was also an editor/writer at Little Golden Books.

Today, she is the executive editor, Media, of Scholastic Classroom Magazines writing about pop-culture, sports, news, and special events. Morreale lives in New York City and is entertained daily by her two Maine coon cats, Cher and Sullivan.